SELECTION OF
DRIED BEANS AND PASTA

VEGETABLE AU GRATIN
AND WHITE LEMON SAUCE

Natural Foods Cookbook

Photographer
Reg Morrison

Editor
Elizabeth Sewell

Food for
Photography
Elizabeth Sewell
Judy Barr

Designer
Hugh McLeod

Published by Paul Hamlyn Pty. Ltd.,
176 South Creek Rd., Dee Why West,
New South Wales, 2099
First Published 1972
©Copyright Paul Hamlyn Pty. Ltd. 1972
Printed by Lee Fung, Hong Kong
Registry number 0 600 07018 2

Natural
Foods
Cookbook

Anna Lee

HG

Paul Hamlyn
Sydney London
New York Toronto

Introduction

Natural Foods Cookbook is primarily a recipe book for people who wish to vary their diet occasionally with a vegetarian dish instead of, or as an accompaniment to, meat.

The human body is a machine which, when given the correct food, is capable not only of resisting disease, but of repairing and restoring itself. Many illnesses experienced by adults in the Western World today, are caused by careless eating habits during childhood and adolescence.

Past generations were quite unaware of the science of nutrition. More and more, health authorities throughout the world are releasing literature to school children in the hope that their children, at least, will live a life free from some of the illnesses affecting today's over-indulged societies.

The family cook can influence the general health and even the life span of a family. A new and healthy way of life awaits everyone who is willing to take the time to prepare protein and vitamin-rich food.

Many recipes in this book contain canned ingredients. My reason for including them is that many housewives lead a busy life and have limited time for cooking family meals, also, some foods are not readily available in all areas. However, whenever possible, substitute fresh ingredients for the canned ones.

I have collected my recipes from many countries and hope you enjoy Natural Food's Cookbook and your new way of life.

Anna Lee

Contents

Guide to Weights and Measures

The weights and fluid measures used throughout this book refer to those of THE STANDARDS ASSOCIATION OF AUSTRALIA. All spoon measurements are level unless otherwise stated. A good set of scales, a graduated Australian Standard measuring cup and a set of Australian Standard measuring spoons will be most helpful. These are available at leading hardware stores.

The Australian Standard measuring cup has a capacity of 8 fluid ounces.
The Australian Standard tablespoon has a capacity of 20 millilitres.
The Australian Standard teaspoon has a capacity of 5 millilitres.
The British imperial pint (used in Australia) has a volume of 20 fluid ounces.

AMERICAN CANADIAN WEIGHTS

AMERICAN weights and measures are the same except for the tablespoon.

Housewives in AMERICA and CANADA using this book should remember that the AUSTRALIAN standard measuring tablespoon has a capacity of 20 millilitres, whereas the AMERICAN/CANADIAN standard measuring tablespoon has a capacity of 15 millilitres, therefore all tablespoon measures should be taken generously in AMERICA and CANADA.

It is also important to know that the imperial pint (20 fluid ounces) is used in Australia, whereas the AMERICAN/CANADIAN pint has a volume of 16 fluid ounces.

Metric Guide

Because there is no exact conversion between metric and imperial units, we suggest the housewife replaces 1 ounce with 25 grams and 1 fluid ounce with 25 millilitres.

In order to preserve the correct ratio of ingredients in a recipe, strict conversion should not be applied. Each imperial measure—whether a pound, pint or cup, should be related to the base unit of the imperial system—the ounce or fluid ounce. The number of ounces and fluid ounces should be multiplied by 25 to give the metric quantities, thereby preserving the proportions.

This has been done in the table provided.

Ounces and Fluid Ounces	Grams and Millilitres
1	25
2	50
3	75
4	100
5	125
6	150
7	175
8	200
10	250
12	300
16 (1 pound)	400
20 (1 pint)	500

Liquid proportions should be adjusted if necessary to maintain correct consistencies.

 metric usage follows metric conversion board recommendation

Oven Temperature Guide

This is an approximate guide only. Different makes of stoves vary and even the same make of stove can give slightly different individual results at the same temperature. If in doubt with your particular stove, do refer to your own manufacturer's temperature chart. It is impossible in a general book to be exact for every stove, but the following is a good average guide in every case.

The following chart also gives approximate conversions from degrees Fahrenheit to degrees Celsius (formerly known as Centigrade). This chart can be used for conversion of recipes which give oven temperatures in metric measures.

Description of Oven	Thermostat Setting °F		°C
	Automatic Electric	Gas	
Cool	200	200	100
Very slow	250	250	120
Slow	300–325	300	150–160
Moderately slow	325–350	325	160–170
Moderate	350–375	350	170–190
Moderately hot	375–400	375	190–200
Hot	400–450	400	200–230
Very hot	450–500	450	230–260

Health
Hints

Eat slowly in a relaxed atmosphere, this will aid digestion.

Eat small quantities of protein and vitamin-rich food instead of large helpings of over-refined food.

Eat a good breakfast. Include fruit juice or raw fruit, wheat germ, fresh wholemeal bread and milk.

Refrain from eating a large meal at the end of the day before retiring. You will sleep soundly if you avoid stimulating foods such as tea and coffee.

Try to cook sufficient food for one meal only, reheated food has little nutriment value.

The human body needs a certain amount of salt in order to function properly, but few of us are aware that most vegetables contain salt and that when cooked correctly, they require little, if any, extra. There are varieties of salt available which have been extracted from vegetables, these are beneficial to your health.

Store food correctly in sealed containers. Keep perishable food in the refrigerator and non-perishable food in a dark, dry cupboard.

Use stainless steel or pyrex glass saucepans rather than aluminium ones, as the latter leave traces of aluminium in the food.

Always rinse eating utensils with clear water after washing up with detergents.

Eat raw, fresh fruits and vegetables whenever possible. Buy in small quantities as they lose their vitamin content quickly.

Clean vegetables with a strong brush before cooking in order to remove dirt and harmful chemicals deposited by sprays.

Whenever possible, leave outer leaves and skin on vegetables and fruits as these often discarded parts are a valuable source of vitamins. When vegetables are peeled, remove immediate skin only.

When using frozen ingredients, follow instructions on the packet, this will ensure food does not lose valuable nutriments.

Use water in which vegetables have been cooked, for home-made soups and stock.

Home-made soups are nutritious. Simmer until ingredients are tender and eat immediately, do not boil for hours or re-heat several times.

Eat raw sugar and honey instead of refined sugar whenever possible.

Eat wholemeal flour, wholemeal spaghetti and brown rice instead of refined varieties.

Use polyunsaturated oils and margarines whenever possible.

Soups

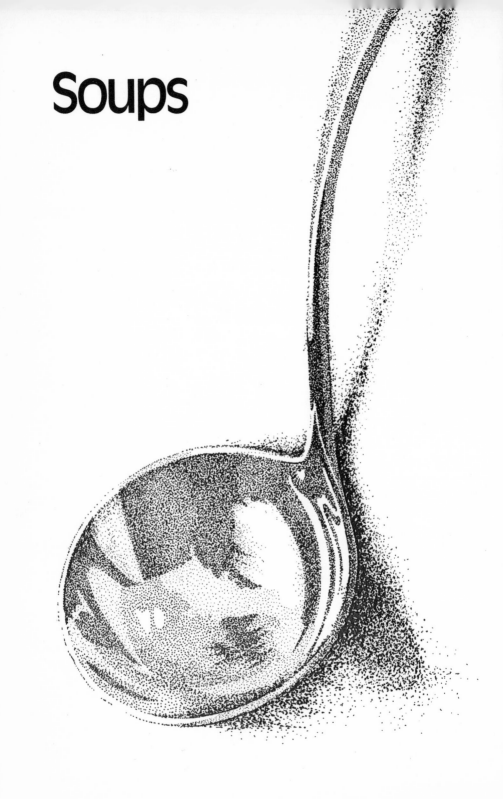

Chilled Bortsch

Serves: 4

2 young beetroot, peeled
5 cups water
1 teaspoon salt
1 cucumber, peeled
2 tomatoes, peeled
5–6 spring onions
sour cream and chopped fresh dill for serving

Dice beetroot. Pour water into saucepan, bring to the boil, add salt and beetroot, cook until tender, cool.

Finely chop cucumber, tomatoes and spring onions, add to soup, mix thoroughly and chill.

Top each bowl of soup with sour cream and chopped dill before serving.

Cherry Soup

Serves: 4

1 × 16 oz can cherries or 1 lb fresh cherries, stewed
1¼ cups milk
2 tablespoons (1 oz) sugar or 2 tablespoons honey
4 cups water
freshly grated nutmeg
whipped cream for serving (optional)

Drain cherries and reserve syrup. Halve cherries and remove stones. Place in a bowl with reserved syrup, milk and sugar, stand overnight.

Next day, combine cherry mixture and water in a saucepan, bring to the boil. Remove from heat and cool. Add nutmeg and chill thoroughly. If liked, top each bowl of soup with a spoonful of cream before serving.

Barley Soup with Vegetables

Serves: 4

$\frac{1}{4}$ cup barley
5 cups water
1 teaspoon salt
1 carrot, chopped
1 stalk celery, sliced
1 packet dehydrated vegetable soup
1 onion, finely chopped
1 tablespoon vegetable oil
finely chopped parsley for serving

Soak barley in cold water overnight, drain.

Pour water into a saucepan and add salt, barley, carrot, celery and vegetable soup. Cover and simmer gently for 1 hour, add mushroom soup.

Fry onion in hot oil until golden, add to soup and stir thoroughly. Simmer for a further 15 minutes. Sprinkle each serving with chopped parsley.

Thick Bean Soup

Serves: 4

2 oz lima beans
2 oz red kidney beans
5 cups water
1 teaspoon salt
2 oz barley
1 carrot, chopped
1 stalk celery, sliced
2 mushroom stock cubes
finely chopped mint or parsley for serving

Soak lima beans and kidney beans in cold water overnight, drain.

Next day, bring water to the boil, add salt, beans, barley, carrots and celery and simmer for approximately 30 minutes. Add mushroom stock cubes, stir well and simmer soup gently until beans are tender.

Sprinkle each serving with chopped mint or parsley.

SELECTION OF FRESH VEGETABLES

MINESTRONE

Russian Bortsch

Serves: 4

1 beetroot, peeled and diced
1 carrot, peeled and diced
4 tablespoons vegetable oil
5 cups water
1 teaspoon salt
1 potato, peeled and diced
2–3 peppercorns
2 bay leaves
3 tomatoes, skinned and chopped
1 onion, chopped
6 mushrooms, chopped
1 × 10 oz can condensed tomato soup
1 cup shredded cabbage

Sauté beetroot and carrot lightly in half the oil.

Place water, salt, potato, peppercorns, bay leaves, tomatoes and sautéed beetroot and carrot in a large saucepan, cover and simmer gently for 20 minutes.

In a smaller saucepan, fry onion and mushrooms in remaining oil until golden brown, add tomato soup and mix well. Add to large saucepan of soup with cabbage, simmer for a further 10–15 minutes. Adjust seasoning if necessary, remove bay leaves before serving.

Minestrone

Serves: 4

1–2 cloves garlic, crushed
$\frac{1}{2}$ cup finely chopped carrot
1 onion, chopped
1 oz butter or margarine
5 cups hot water
1 teaspoon salt
freshly ground pepper
2 teaspoons concentrated yeast extract
$\frac{1}{2}$ cup wholemeal macaroni
1 cup shredded cabbage
grated Parmesan cheese for serving

Sauté garlic, carrot and onion in butter for 5 minutes. Add water, soup mix, salt, pepper and yeast extract. Cover and simmer gently for approximately 1 hour.

Add macaroni, celery and cabbage and cook for a further 15 minutes or until macaroni is tender.

Sprinkle each serving with Parmesan cheese.

Rice and Tomato Soup

Serves: 4

5 cups water
1 teaspoon salt
$\frac{1}{2}$ cup brown rice
1 carrot, finely chopped
1 large tomato, peeled
$\frac{1}{4}$ oz butter or margarine
freshly ground pepper
finely chopped parsley for serving

Bring water to boiling point, add salt, rice and carrot. Cover and simmer gently for 20 minutes.

Chop tomato and add to soup, cook a further 10 minutes. Add butter and pepper, adjust seasoning if necessary. Serve immediately, sprinkled with parsley.

Thick Vegetable Soup

Serves: 4

$\frac{1}{2}$ cup split peas
$\frac{1}{2}$ cup dehydrated soup mix
2 stalks celery, sliced
2 carrots, chopped
3 bay leaves
6 cups water
salt and pepper
1 × 16 oz can condensed mushroom soup
1 tablespoon vegetable oil
$\frac{1}{2}$ onion, finely chopped

Soak split peas overnight in cold water, drain.

Place split peas, soup mix, celery, carrots, bay leaves, water and salt and pepper in a large saucepan. Bring to the boil, cover and simmer gently for $1\frac{1}{2}$ hours. Add mushroom soup and simmer for a further 30 minutes.

Meanwhile, heat oil in a frying pan, add onion and sauté until golden brown, add to soup. Adjust seasoning if necessary and remove bay leaves from soup before serving.

Main
Courses

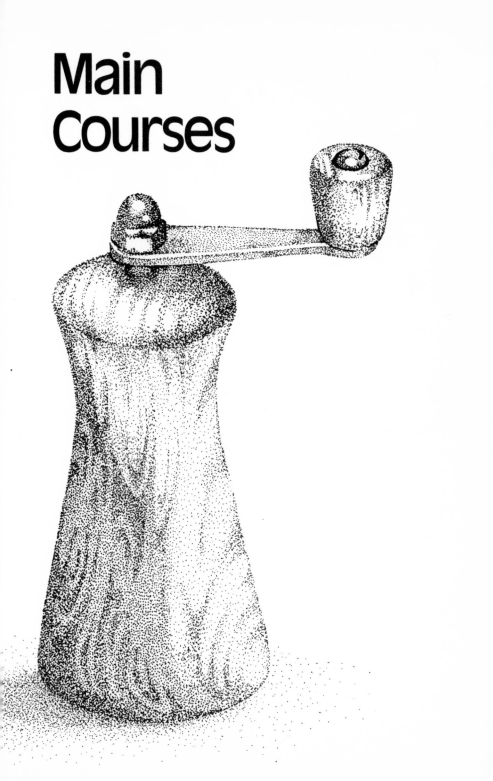

Asparagus Cheese Toast

Serves: 4

4 slices toast, buttered
1 × 16 oz can asparagus spears, drained
4 tablespoons grated Cheddar cheese

Cut toast into fingers, place a spear of asparagus on each, sprinkle with grated cheese.

Cook under a hot grill until cheese is golden brown. Serve immediately.

Beans and Cauliflower Chinese Style

Serves: 4

8 oz French beans
$\frac{1}{4}$ cauliflower
4 tablespoons peanut oil
1 clove garlic, crushed
12 blanched almonds
1 teaspoon sugar
1 teaspoon paprika pepper
salt and pepper
3 tablespoons water

Slice beans and break cauliflower into flowerettes. Cook together in boiling salted water for 5 minutes, drain.

Heat oil in a large frying pan, add garlic and almonds and fry until golden brown. Add beans, cauliflower, sugar, paprika pepper and salt and pepper to taste. Mix gently together over a low heat for approximately 5 minutes. Add water and cook for a further 5 minutes. Serve as a vegetable or on hot buttered toast.

Bean Fiesta

Serves: 4

1 green pepper
1 red pepper
2 hot chillies
2 tablespoons vegetable oil
1 large brown onion, finely chopped
1 × 10 oz can soya beans
1 × 9½ oz can bean sprouts
pinch of ground nutmeg
salt and pepper

Seed and finely chop peppers and chillies.

Heat oil in a large frying pan, sauté onion until golden brown. Add soya beans, bean sprouts, peppers, chillies, nutmeg and salt and pepper to taste, mix together thoroughly. Cook for approximately 10–15 minutes. Serve with a green salad.

Chilli Beans

Serves: 4

2 tablespoons vegetable oil
1 small white onion, finely chopped
1 × 10 oz can red kidney beans
2 hot chillies, seeded and finely sliced
salt
freshly ground black pepper
boiled brown rice for serving

Heat oil in a frying pan, sauté onion until golden
brown. Add beans and chillies and season to taste
with salt and pepper. Mix together thoroughly and
cook gently for approximately 5 minutes. Serve
immediately with brown rice.

Kidney Bean Casserole

Time: 20–30 minutes
Temperature: 350–375 °F
Serves: 4

1 oz butter or margarine
1 large onion, chopped
3 large tomatoes, chopped
8 oz peas, cooked
1 × 10 oz can red kidney beans
salt and pepper
4 potatoes, cooked
extra $\frac{1}{2}$ oz butter or margarine
2 tablespoons finely chopped parsley for garnish

Heat butter in a saucepan, add onion and tomatoes and cook for 10 minutes. Add peas, kidney beans and season with salt and pepper, cook for a further 5 minutes.

Slice potatoes and place a layer in a greased ovenproof casserole. Cover with tomato mixture and top with another layer of potatoes. Dot with extra butter. Cook in a moderate oven for 20–30 minutes or until hot.

Garnish with finely chopped parsley. Serve with a green salad.

Peasant Beans and Rice

Serves: 4

2 cups black beans or lentils
1 clove garlic, crushed
1 onion, halved
salt and pepper
2 oz butter or margarine
boiled brown rice and finely chopped parsley or
dill for serving

Soak beans or lentils in cold water overnight, drain.
Place in boiling water with garlic, onion and salt
and pepper, cover and simmer gently until tender.
Drain and top each serving with a knob of butter.

Combine rice and chopped parsley and serve with
the beans.

Lima Beans and Tomatoes

Serves: 4

1 × 15 oz can peeled tomatoes
1 mushroom stock cube
1 cup hot water
4 tablespoons vegetable oil
2 peppers, seeded and chopped
1 lb lima beans, cooked
1 × 6¾ oz can champignons, drained
salt and pepper

Strain tomatoes and chop roughly. Reserve tomato juice. Dissolve mushroom stock cube in hot water.

Heat oil in a fireproof casserole and cook peppers and tomatoes for 10 minutes. Add reserved tomato juice, lima beans, mushroom stock and champignons and season to taste with salt and pepper. Cook for a further 10 minutes.

Serve with a tossed green salad.

Savoury Lima Beans

Serves: 4

8 oz lima beans
1 oz butter or margarine
2 peppers, seeded and chopped
1 onion, chopped
4 bay leaves
1 × 7¾ oz can tomato purée
2 teaspoons paprika pepper
salt
freshly ground pepper

Soak lima beans in cold water overnight, drain.
Cook in boiling salted water until tender, drain.

Melt butter in a frying pan, add peppers, onion and
bay leaves, sauté gently for 10 minutes. Add beans,
tomato purée and paprika pepper, season to taste
with salt and pepper, mix well. Cook for a further
10–15 minutes or until hot. Remove bay leaves
before serving.

Serve with a green vegetable or salad.

Chinese Cabbage

Serves: 4

$\frac{1}{2}$ large cabbage
1 tablespoon vegetable oil
1 clove garlic, crushed
1 teaspoon raw sugar
salt and pepper
pinch of paprika pepper
4 tablespoons water
finely chopped almonds or fresh root ginger
(optional)

Shred cabbage finely.

Heat oil in a large frying pan and fry garlic until golden. Add cabbage, sugar, salt and pepper, paprika pepper and water, cover and cook for approximately 5 minutes. Remove lid and stirring occasionally, cook cabbage until lightly browned. Adjust seasonings if necessary and add almonds or ginger if desired. Serve with Spicy Baked Potatoes (see page 44).

Note: If preferred, French beans, cauliflower or spinach may be substituted for the cabbage.

Cabbage Hot Pot

(Tushinaya Kapusta)

Serves: 4

$\frac{1}{2}$ small cabbage
1 large onion
3 carrots
4 tablespoons vegetable oil
3 bay leaves
1 × 15 oz can sauerkraut, drained
salt and pepper

Shred cabbage and finely chop onion and carrots.

Heat oil in a large saucepan and sauté onion and carrot until onion is golden brown. Add cabbage, bay leaves, sauerkraut and season to taste with salt and pepper. Cover saucepan and simmer gently for approximately 15 minutes or until vegetables are tender.

Serve with mashed potatoes, peas and grilled tomatoes.

Cabbage Rolls

Serves: 4

8 cabbage leaves
2 tablespoons vegetable oil
½ onion, chopped
1 pepper, seeded and chopped
3 spring onions, chopped
2 large tomatoes, chopped
2 cups cooked brown rice
1 cup finely sliced French beans, cooked
salt and pepper
Sauce:
1 tablespoon vegetable oil
½ onion, chopped
1 × 15 oz can condensed tomato soup
3 tablespoons sour cream
1 tablespoon Worcestershire sauce
2 bay leaves
salt and pepper

Pour boiling water over cabbage leaves to soften, drain.

Heat oil in a saucepan, add onion, pepper, spring onions and tomatoes, cook until tender. Add rice and beans, mix thoroughly and season to taste with salt and pepper.

Divide mixture into 8 portions and place a portion on each cabbage leaf. Roll up, folding in the ends, secure each roll with fine string or cocktail sticks. Place in a large saucepan. Pour sauce over Cabbage Rolls and simmer gently for 20–30 minutes. Remove bay leaves before serving.

Sauce: Heat oil in a saucepan, add onion and fry until golden brown. Add remaining ingredients and simmer for 10 minutes.

INGREDIENTS FOR MAKING
CURRY FIJI

BAKED EGGPLANT AND PASTA

Fried Cauliflower Sprigs

Serves: 4

1 cauliflower
2 teaspoons caraway seeds
juice of $\frac{1}{2}$ lemon
oil for frying

Batter:
1 cup (4 oz) plain flour
$\frac{3}{4}$ cup milk
salt and pepper

Break cauliflower into flowerettes. Add cauliflower, caraway seeds and lemon juice to a saucepan of boiling salted water and cook until just tender, drain. Dip cauliflower in batter and deep fry in hot oil until golden brown. Drain on absorbent paper and serve immediately.

Batter: Sieve flour into a mixing bowl. Stirring continuously, gradually add milk until a smooth batter is formed, add salt and pepper. Stand for 30 minutes before using.

Curry Fiji

Serves: 4

4 oz ghee
2 large brown onions, chopped
3 large potatoes, diced
8 oz French beans, sliced
1 lb zucchini, sliced
2 cups stock or water and vegetable stock cubes
1–2 tablespoons curry paste (according to taste)
2 × 10 oz cans red kidney beans
2 tablespoons vegetable oil
8 oz mushrooms, sliced
salt and pepper

Heat ghee in a large saucepan, add onions and sauté until golden brown. Add potatoes and French beans, mix thoroughly and cook for 15 minutes. Add zucchini, stock, curry paste and red kidney beans, cook for a further 10 minutes.

In the meantime, heat oil in a frying pan and sauté mushrooms for 5 minutes. Add to ingedients in saucepan, season to taste with salt and pepper and mix thoroughly.

Serve curry with pappadums and a green salad.

Note: This curry improves in flavour when cooked in advance and reheated just before serving.

Soya Bean Curry

Serves: 4

4 tablespoons vegetable oil
2 onions, finely chopped
2–3 tablespoons curry paste or powder (according to taste)
4 tablespoons (2 oz) plain wholemeal flour
$2\frac{1}{2}$ cups water
2 tablespoons fruit chutney
8 oz peas, cooked
1 × 10 oz can soya beans

Accompaniments:
2 large bananas
2 tablespoons desiccated coconut
1 small cucumber
4 tablespoons yoghurt
3–4 slices pineapple
boiled brown rice

Heat oil in a saucepan, add onion and sauté until golden brown. Add curry paste and flour and stir until smooth. Add water and stirring continuously, bring to the boil, simmer for 5 minutes. Pour approximately one-third of the curry sauce into another saucepan and add fruit chutney, keep warm.

To remaining curry sauce add peas and soya beans, cook gently for approximately 10 minutes.

Serve the two curries with accompaniments.

Accompaniments: Slice banana and toss in coconut, place in a small bowl.
Peel and thinly slice cucumber, combine with yoghurt and place in a small bowl.
Cut pineapple into chunks and place in a small bowl.

Baked Eggplant and Pasta

Time: 20–30 minutes
Temperature: 350–375°F
Serves: 4

1 eggplant
salt
1 oz butter or margarine
1 onion, chopped
1 × 16 oz can peeled tomatoes
extra salt
freshly ground pepper
8 oz wholemeal spaghetti
milk and wheat germ for coating
vegetable oil for frying
2 oz Cheddar cheese, grated

Slice eggplant, sprinkle with salt and stand for several hours.

Melt butter in a saucepan, add onion and sauté until golden brown. Add tomatoes, extra salt and freshly ground pepper to taste. Simmer for approximately 10 minutes.

Cook spaghetti in boiling salted water until just tender, drain.

Dip slices of eggplant in milk and coat with wheat germ. Heat oil in a frying pan and cook eggplant until golden brown on both sides.

In a greased ovenproof casserole, layer eggplant, spaghetti and sauce until all ingredients are used. Sprinkle grated cheese on top. Cook in a moderate oven for 20–30 minutes or until hot and golden brown on top.

Eggplant and Vegetable Casserole

Time: 30 minutes
Temperature: 350–375°F
Serves: 4

1 eggplant
salt
milk and wheat germ for coating
1 × 16 oz can meat substitute patties
vegetable oil for frying
8 oz French beans, sliced
2 cups peas
½ oz ghee
1 onion, chopped
1 tomato, chopped
extra salt
freshly ground pepper
1 cup stock or water and onion stock cube

Thinly slice eggplant, sprinkle with salt and stand for several hours. Dip eggplant in milk and coat with wheat germ. Dip meat substitute patties in milk and coat with wheat germ. Heat oil in a frying pan and fry eggplant and meat substitute until golden brown on both sides, drain and keep warm.

Cook beans and peas together in boiling salted water until tender, drain.

Heat ghee in a frying pan, fry onion until golden brown. Add tomato and season to taste with extra salt and freshly ground pepper. Add peas, beans and stock, mix together thoroughly. Place in an ovenproof casserole and cook in a moderate oven for 15 minutes. Remove casserole from oven and add layers of eggplant and meat substitute. Replace in oven for a further 15 minutes. Serve immediately.

Macaroni and Peas

Serves: 4

2 lb peas
$\frac{1}{4}$ cup vegetable oil
2 large brown onions, finely chopped
2 cups water
salt and pepper
12 oz wholemeal macaroni

Shell peas.

Heat oil in a saucepan, add onions and sauté until golden brown. Add peas, cover and simmer for 10 minutes. Add water and salt and pepper to taste, simmer gently until peas are tender.

Meanwhile, cook macaroni in boiling salted water until tender, drain. Mix macaroni and peas together and serve piping hot.

Mexican Delight

Time: 20–30 minutes
Temperature: 350–375°F
Serves: 4

½ oz butter or margarine
½ white onion, chopped
1 × 7 oz can pimientos, finely sliced
1 × 15 oz can whole kernel sweet corn
1 × 15 oz can peeled tomatoes
2 tablespoons tomato purée
1 teaspoon raw sugar
salt and pepper
1 × 10 oz can asparagus tips
1 cup grated Cheddar cheese

Heat butter in a flameproof casserole, sauté onion and pimientos for a few minutes. Add sweet corn, tomatoes, tomato purée, sugar and salt and pepper to taste. Mix together thoroughly, finally add asparagus. Sprinkle cheese on top.

Place in a moderate oven and cook for approximately 20–30 minutes or until casserole is hot and golden brown on top. Serve with a green vegetable or salad.

Mushroom Casserole

Time: 20–30 minutes
Temperature: 400–450 °F
Serves: 4

1 lb mushrooms
1 oz butter or margarine
1 large onion, chopped
2 cups peas
salt and pepper
4 cups cooked brown rice

Wipe and slice mushrooms.

Heat butter in a large frying pan, add onion and sauté until golden, remove from heat. Add mushrooms and peas, mix together thoroughly, season to taste with salt and pepper. In a greased ovenproof casserole, alternate layers of rice and mixed vegetables.

Place in a hot oven and cook for 20–30 minutes or until vegetables are tender.

Mushrooms with Cream

Serves: 4

1 lb mushrooms
½ oz butter or margarine
juice of ½ lemon
salt and pepper
¾ cup cream
2 tablespoons finely chopped parsley

Wipe and slice mushrooms.

Heat butter in a frying pan and add mushrooms, lemon juice and salt and pepper. Stirring occasionally, cook for 5 minutes. Add cream and parsley and simmer for a further 5 minutes. Adjust seasonings if necessary and serve immediately on hot buttered toast or as a vegetable.

41

Mushroom Pizza

Time: 20–25 minutes
Temperature: 375–400°F
Serves: 4

2 cups (8 oz) plain wholemeal flour
½ teaspoon salt
1 teaspoon sugar
¼ oz active dry yeast
⅔ cup warm water

Topping:
1 × 5 oz can tomato paste
6 tablespoons tomato sauce
1 tablespoon Worcestershire sauce
pinch of dried oregano
8 oz mushrooms, sliced
1 × 7 oz can pimientos, sliced
1 small white onion, chopped
4 oz mozzarella cheese, sliced

Place 1 cup of the sieved flour, salt, sugar and yeast in a mixing bowl. Add water and beat for 2 minutes in a mixer or 300 strokes by hand. Add remaining flour and mix together until smooth. Cover bowl with a cloth and prove for 10 minutes. Spread dough evenly with spoon or oiled fingers over a greased 12-inch pizza tin.

Place topping on pizza. Cook in a moderately hot oven for 20–25 minutes or until cheese is golden brown and bubbly. Cut into wedges and serve immediately.

Topping: Combine tomato paste, tomato sauce, Worcestershire sauce and oregano, spread over dough. Cover with mushrooms, pimientos, onion and cheese.

Noodles with Onions

Serves: 4

½ cup vegetable oil
4 large onions, finely sliced
1 cup water
1 teaspoon salt
freshly ground black pepper
1 lb noodles
butter for serving

Heat oil in a saucepan, add onions and fry gently for approximately 15 minutes or until golden, remove from heat. When cool, add water and salt and pepper, return to heat and stirring occasionally, simmer for approximately 30 minutes or until water is reduced.

Meanwhile, cook noodles in boiling salted water until tender, drain. Serve onions over noodles and top each serving with a knob of butter.

Spicy Baked Potatoes

Time: 1¼ hours
Temperature: 400–450°F
Serves: 4

4 old potatoes
2 oz butter or margarine
2 stalks celery, finely chopped
1 large tomato, skinned and chopped
salt
freshly ground pepper

Scrub and dry potatoes, prick with a fork. Bake in a hot oven for approximately 1 hour or until tender.

Cut a slice from the top of each potato and scoop out the soft centre, place in a bowl. Add butter, celery, tomato and salt and pepper to taste. Mix together thoroughly. Place mixture back in potato skins and replace in oven for a further 15 minutes or until hot. Serve with a green vegetable or salad.

Fried Potato Balls

Serves: 4

4 large potatoes
½ cup (2 oz) plain wholemeal flour
salt
freshly ground pepper
little milk to moisten
½ cup vegetable oil
1 onion, chopped

Scrub potatoes well. Cook in boiling salted water until tender. Drain and place in a mixing bowl. Mash potatoes, add flour, salt and pepper to taste and just enough milk to form a firm dough. Roll into small round balls.

Heat oil in a large frying pan and fry onion and potato balls until golden brown. Drain on absorbent paper and serve with a green salad.

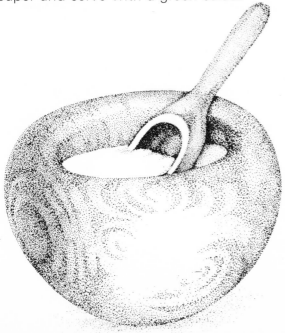

Paprika Potato Casserole

Time: 20–30 minutes
Temperature: 350–375 °F
Serves: 4

6 old potatoes
½ oz butter or margarine
½ cup milk
2 tablespoons cream
salt and pepper
1 × 10 oz packet frozen broccoli or 10 oz fresh broccoli
1 cup peas, cooked
1 × 15½ oz can condensed mushroom soup
½ cup wheat germ
2 oz cheese, grated
1 teaspoon paprika pepper

Peel potatoes, cook in boiling salted water until tender, drain and mash. Add butter, milk, cream and salt and pepper to taste, mix together thoroughly.

Cook broccoli in boiling salted water until tender, drain. Place broccoli and peas in a greased ovenproof casserole, cover with mushroom soup. Sprinkle with wheat germ and cheese and cover with mashed potato. Sprinkle with paprika pepper.

Cook in a moderate oven for approximately 20–30 minutes or until hot and golden brown on top.

Potato and Carrot Combination

(Jarkoyer)

Serves: 4

6 old potatoes
3 carrots
3 bay leaves
1 teaspoon salt
freshly ground black pepper
$\frac{1}{2}$ teaspoon paprika pepper
4 tablespoons vegetable oil
1 large onion, finely chopped
$1\frac{1}{4}$ cups water

Peel and quarter potatoes and carrots. Place in a saucepan with bay leaves and seasonings.

Heat oil in a frying pan and sauté onion until golden brown, add water and simmer for 2 minutes. Pour into saucepan with vegetables and toss together gently. Cover and simmer gently for 30–45 minutes or until vegetables are tender.
While cooking, stir occasionally and add a little extra water if vegetables appear to be dry. Remove bay leaves and serve with a green vegetable or salad.

Potato Cakes

Serves: 4

4 old potatoes
1 onion
2 tablespoons (1 oz) plain wholemeal flour
1 teaspoon salt
freshly ground pepper
2 oz butter or margarine
sour cream for serving

Peel and grate potatoes and onion, drain off liquid. Place in a mixing bowl with flour and salt and pepper, mix together thoroughly.

Melt butter in a frying pan and when hot, place spoonfuls of mixture in pan, fry on both sides until golden brown. Place on a plate in a warm place until all the mixture is used.

Top with sour cream before serving.

MUSHROOM PIZZA

SPICY BAKED POTATOES

Potato Pie

Time: 20 minutes
Temperature: 400–450°F
Serves: 4

1 lb potatoes
2 tomatoes
2 oz butter or margarine
1 onion, finely chopped
$\frac{1}{2}$ cup (2 oz) plain wholemeal flour
1$\frac{1}{2}$ cups milk
salt and pepper
1 cup grated Parmesan cheese

Peel potatoes and cook in boiling salted water
until tender, drain. Dice and place in a greased
ovenproof casserole. Slice tomatoes and place in a
layer over the potatoes.

Melt butter in a saucepan, sauté onion until golden
brown. Add flour and blend until smooth. Add
milk and stirring continuously, bring to the boil.
Season to taste with salt and pepper and add half
the cheese, stir until melted. Pour sauce over
vegetables in casserole and sprinkle remaining
cheese on top.

Cook in a hot oven for approximately 20 minutes
or until golden brown on top.

Fried Rice

Serves: 4

1½ cups brown rice
4 tablespoons vegetable oil
6–8 spring onions, chopped
1 large pepper, seeded and chopped
2 carrots, chopped
1 tablespoon Worcestershire sauce
salt and pepper

Cook rice in boiling salted water for approximately 25 minutes or until tender, drain and rinse thoroughly.

Heat oil in a large frying pan and sauté spring onions, pepper and carrots until tender. Add rice, Worcestershire sauce and season to taste with salt and pepper. Mix with a fork and when hot, serve immediately.

Risotto

Serves: 4

6 oz butter or margarine
2 brown onions, sliced
1 clove garlic, crushed
12 oz brown rice
salt and pepper
4 cups stock or water and vegetable stock cubes
8 oz button mushrooms, sliced
3–4 tablespoons grated Parmesan cheese

Place 4 oz of the butter in a large saucepan, add onions and sauté until golden. Add garlic, rice, salt and pepper and half the stock. Simmer gently until stock has been absorbed. Add remaining stock and continue to cook gently until rice is tender and stock has been absorbed again.

Meanwhile, sauté mushrooms in remaining butter until tender. Add to rice and stir gently with a fork, adjust seasoning if necessary.

Sprinkle with cheese and serve immediately.

Spaghetti with Tomato Sauce

Serves: 4

2 oz butter or margarine
1 large onion, finely chopped
1 large pepper, seeded and finely chopped
1 × 15 oz can peeled tomatoes or 6 large fresh tomatoes
pinch of dried oregano
salt and pepper
1 × 12 oz packet wholemeal spaghetti
grated Parmesan cheese for serving

Melt butter in a frying pan and add onion and pepper, fry gently until onion is golden brown. Chop tomatoes and add to frying pan with oregano and salt and pepper to taste. Simmer for approximately 20 minutes or until pepper is tender.

Meanwhile, cook spaghetti in boiling salted water until tender, drain.

Serve sauce over spaghetti and top with grated cheese.

Tomato and Garlic Spaghetti

Serves: 4
$\frac{1}{3}$ cup vegetable oil
2 cloves garlic, crushed
1 × 16 oz can peeled tomatoes
$\frac{1}{4}$ teaspoon dried oregano
salt and pepper
1 × 12 oz packet wholemeal spaghetti
grated Parmesan cheese for serving

Heat oil in a saucepan, add garlic and fry until golden. Add tomatoes, oregano and salt and pepper to taste. Simmer gently for 15 minutes.

Meanwhile, cook spaghetti in boiling salted water until tender, drain.

Serve sauce over spaghetti, sprinkle with Parmesan cheese.

Spinach Europa

Serves: 4

1 lb spinach
2 oz butter or margarine
2 good tablespoons (1 oz) plain wholemeal flour
1¼ cups milk
salt and pepper
1 clove garlic, crushed
½ cup grated Parmesan cheese

Wash spinach thoroughly and shred. Melt half the butter in a large saucepan, add spinach, cover and cook gently for approximately 10–12 minutes or until tender. Drain well and keep warm.

Melt remaining butter in a saucepan, add flour and blend until smooth. Add milk and stirring continuously, bring to the boil. Season to taste with salt and pepper, add garlic and simmer for 5 minutes.

Mix spinach and sauce together, place in a fireproof casserole and sprinkle with cheese. Brown under a hot grill and serve with Potato and Carrot Combination (see page 47).

Sweet Corn and Asparagus Casserole

Time: 20–30 minutes
Temperature: 350–375°F
Serves: 4

1 oz butter or margarine
1 small onion, chopped
1 green pepper, seeded and chopped
1 × 16 oz can whole kernel sweet corn
1 × 10 oz can asparagus tips
1 × 7 oz can pimientos, finely sliced
salt and pepper
1 cup grated Cheddar cheese

Heat butter in a flameproof casserole and sauté onion and pepper until tender. Add sweet corn, asparagus, pimientos and salt and pepper to taste.

Sprinkle cheese on top and place in a moderate oven for 20–30 minutes or until golden brown on top.

Note: Fresh, cooked sweet corn and asparagus may be used in this recipe.

Grilled Tomatoes with Cheese

Serves: 4

4 tomatoes
salt
freshly ground pepper
4 oz Parmesan cheese, grated
1 tablespoon lemon juice
1 tablespoon finely chopped parsley or mint

Cut tomatoes in halves and sprinkle with salt, pepper and Parmesan cheese.

Cook under a hot grill for 5 minutes or until golden brown on top. Sprinkle with lemon juice and parsley. Serve as a vegetable or on hot buttered toast.

Tomato and Onion Savoury

Serves: 4

1 oz butter or margarine
1 large onion, sliced
6 large ripe tomatoes, chopped
pinch of dried oregano
1 teaspoon raw sugar
salt
freshly ground pepper

Heat butter in a saucepan and sauté onion until golden. Add tomatoes, oregano, sugar and salt and pepper to taste. Simmer gently for approximately 15 minutes or until tomatoes are tender.

Serve immediately on hot buttered toast or serve cold as an entrée.

Stuffed Tomatoes

Time: 20–30 minutes
Temperature: 350–375 °F
Serves: 4

4 large firm tomatoes
1 teaspoon salt
½ cup chopped celery
2 tablespoons finely chopped onion
½ green pepper, seeded and finely chopped
¼ cup wheat germ
1½ cups puréed soya beans
freshly ground pepper

Cut a slice from the top of each tomato, remove soft centre and place in a bowl. Sprinkle a little salt inside each tomato case. Add celery, onion, pepper, wheat germ, puréed soy beans and freshly ground pepper to tomato pulp, mix together thoroughly.

Fill tomato cases with mixture and place in a greased, shallow ovenproof casserole. Cook in a moderate oven for 20–30 minutes or until tender. Serve with a green vegetable or salad.

Note: Purée soya beans by passing through a sieve or blender.

Boiled Vegetable Dinner

Serves: 4

6 potatoes
1 lb pumpkin
1 cabbage
4 zucchini
Brown Gravy (see page 84)

Peel potatoes and pumpkin and cut pumpkin into large pieces. Cook in a large saucepan of boiling salted water for 15 minutes.

In the meantime, cut cabbage into quarters and secure with fine string or cotton. Add to potatoes and pumpkin with zucchini, cook for a further 15 minutes or until vegetables are tender.

Drain vegetables thoroughly, place in a serving dish and pour Brown Gravy over. Serve immediately.

Vegetables au Gratin

Time: 20–30 minutes
Temperature: 350–375°F
Serves: 4

¼ cauliflower
2 large carrots
8 brussels sprouts
1 cup bean sprouts
juice of ½ lemon
½ cup wheat germ
½ cup grated Cheddar cheese
1 tablespoon finely chopped parsley

Spinach Side Dish:
½ bunch spinach, shredded
2 tablespoons vegetable oil
½ onion, sliced
1 chilli, seeded and sliced
White Lemon Sauce (see page 86) and creamed
potato for serving

Break cauliflower into flowerettes. Peel carrots and
cut into rings, trim brussels sprouts. Cook
cauliflower, carrots and brussels sprouts in boiling
salted water until tender, drain.

Place vegetables and bean sprouts in a greased
ovenproof casserole. Sprinkle with lemon juice,
wheat germ and cheese. Cook in a moderate oven
for 20–30 minutes or until hot and golden brown
on top.

Sprinkle with parsley and serve with prepared
spinach side dish, White Lemon Sauce and
creamed potato.

Spinach Side Dish: Cook spinach in boiling salted water for approximately 10–12 minutes, drain thoroughly.

Heat vegetable oil in a frying pan, sauté onion and chilli for a few minutes, add spinach and mix together thoroughly.

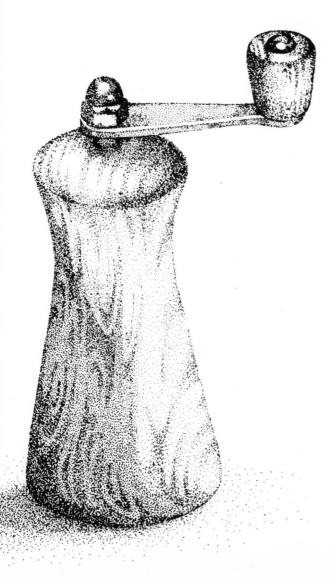

Vegetable Combination

Serves: 4

1 lb new marble potatoes
$\frac{1}{4}$ cup finely chopped parsley or dill
2 oz butter or margarine
1 cup peas
2 cups sliced French beans
2 teaspoons lemon juice
salt and pepper
2 large tomatoes
2 tablespoons grated Cheddar cheese
2 tablespoons finely chopped green olives

Wash potatoes and cook in boiling salted water until tender. Drain and toss with parsley and half the butter, keep warm.

Cook peas and beans together in boiling salted water until tender, drain. Add lemon juice, remaining butter and season to taste with salt and pepper, keep warm.

Cut tomatoes in halves, sprinkle with grated cheese and chopped olives. Cook under a hot grill for approximately 5 minutes. Place vegetables on a serving dish and serve immediately.

Salads

Avocado and Grapefruit Salad

Serves: 4

3 avocado pears, peeled, stoned and sliced
1 grapefruit, peeled and cut into segments
2 oranges, peeled and cut into segments
1 small lettuce
French Dressing (see page 80)

Arrange prepared avocado pears, grapefruit and oranges on crisp lettuce leaves.

Serve French Dressing separately.

Mixed Bean Salad

Serves: 4

1 × 10 oz can red kidney beans
1 × 10 oz can lima beans
8 oz French beans, cooked and sliced
1 onion, finely chopped
2 tomatoes, chopped
French Dressing (see page 80)
lettuce for serving

Drain kidney and lima beans, rinse with cold water.

Place all ingredients in a bowl and pour over French Dressing. Toss together thoroughly and chill.

Serve bean salad on a bed of lettuce.

FRUIT LUNCH SALAD

Kidney Bean Salad

Serves: 4

1 × 10 oz can red kidney beans, drained
$\frac{1}{2}$ cup chopped celery
1 cup chopped sweet pickles
$\frac{1}{2}$ cup stoned, sliced black olives
1 cup mayonnaise
3 tablespoons tomato purée
$\frac{1}{2}$ teaspoon Tabasco sauce
salt and pepper
lettuce for serving
finely chopped parsley for garnish

Rinse beans with cold water, drain. Combine with remaining ingredients, mix well and season to taste with salt and pepper. Chill and serve in lettuce cups, sprinkle with parsley.

Summer Beetroot Salad

Serves: 4

2 large beetroot, cooked
2 large potatoes, cooked
1 small cucumber
6 gherkins, sliced
1 white onion, finely chopped
1 × 16 oz can sauerkraut, drained
French Dressing (see page 80)

Peel and dice beetroot, potatoes and cucumber.
Place in a salad bowl with gherkins, onion and
sauerkraut. Pour over French Dressing and toss
together. Serve immediately.

Coleslaw

Serves: 4

$\frac{1}{2}$ small cabbage, shredded
2 carrots, grated
1 onion, grated
1 clove garlic, crushed (optional)
2–3 stalks celery, sliced
2 tablespoons salad oil
$\frac{1}{2}$ cup mayonnaise
1 teaspoon salt
freshly ground pepper
pinch of sugar

Place all ingredients in a large salad bowl and mix together thoroughly. Serve immediately.

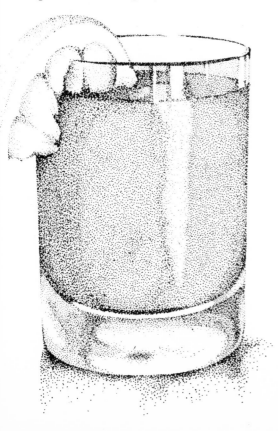

Fruit Lunch Salad

apples
oranges
preserved ginger
dates
raisins
cottage cheese
lettuce and mayonnaise for serving

Core and slice apples. Peel oranges and cut into
segments. Chop ginger and dates. Place raisins,
dates and cottage cheese on lettuce leaves, arrange
sliced apple and orange on top, sprinkle with
ginger. Serve mayonnaise separately.

Garden Salad

Serves: 4

1 lettuce
2 cups diced carrots, cooked
2 cups cauliflower sprigs, cooked
1 cup chopped celery, cooked
1 large cucumber, thinly sliced
3 cups chopped tomatoes
2 oz chopped nuts, toasted

Dressing:
$\frac{1}{2}$ cup soya bean oil
juice of 1 lemon
1 tablespoon finely chopped parsley
1 teaspoon paprika pepper
salt and pepper

Reserve some lettuce leaves to line a salad bowl, shred remaining lettuce.

Combine carrots, cauliflower, celery, cucumber, tomatoes and shredded lettuce, mix well. Place in salad bowl lined with lettuce, chill.

To serve, pour dressing over and sprinkle with nuts. Serve immediately.

Dressing: Combine ingredients in a screw-top jar and shake vigorously.

69

Olive and Grapefruit Salad

Serves: 4

1 grapefruit
1 × 7 oz can pimientos, drained
1 lettuce
1 cup black olives, stoned

Dressing:
$\frac{1}{2}$ cup salad oil
1 tablespoon tarragon vinegar
freshly ground pepper
1 tablespoon lemon juice
pinch of salt
pinch of dry mustard

Peel grapefruit and cut into small pieces. Thinly slice pimientos. Wash lettuce, tear into bite-size pieces and place in a salad bowl. Add grapefruit, pimientos and olives. Pour dressing over salad and serve immediately.

Dressing: Place all ingredients in a screw-top jar and shake vigorously.

Olive Onion Salad

Serves: 4

2 white onions
1 orange
1 green pepper
12 black olives, halved and stoned

Dressing:
2 tablespoons salad oil
1 tablespoon lemon juice
$\frac{1}{2}$ teaspoon dry mustard
$\frac{1}{2}$ teaspoon sugar
salt and pepper

Peel and thinly slice onions and orange. Seed pepper and cut into thin slices. Combine onions, orange, pepper and olives in a serving dish. Pour dressing over and chill before serving.

Dressing: Place all ingredients in a screw-top jar and shake vigorously.

Russian Potato Salad

Serves: 4

6 potatoes, cooked
1½ cups chopped carrots, cooked
2 cups peas, cooked
1 white onion, finely sliced
3 tablespoons salad oil
½ cup mayonnaise
salt and pepper
lettuce leaves, sliced tomato and chopped parsley
or mint for serving

Slice potatoes and place in a large bowl with
carrots, peas and onion. Add oil, mayonnaise and
salt and pepper to taste. Mix together gently.

Serve on a bed of lettuce, garnish with tomato and
parsley.

Yoghurt Potato Salad

Serves: 4

2 lb potatoes, cooked and diced
$\frac{1}{4}$ cup chopped spring onions
12 French beans, cooked and sliced
$\frac{1}{4}$ cup sliced celery
1 cup peas, cooked
1 cup yoghurt
$\frac{1}{2}$ teaspoon salt
$\frac{1}{2}$ teaspoon curry powder
freshly ground pepper

Place all ingredients in a large salad bowl, mix together gently until well combined, chill.

Serve with a green salad.

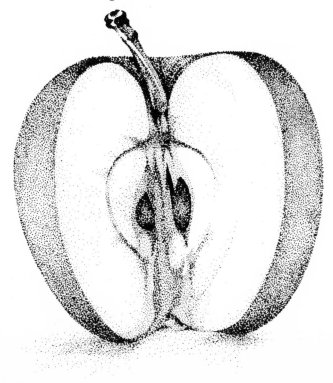

Ginger Rice Salad

Serves: 4

1 large green apple
$\frac{1}{4}$ cup chopped crystallized ginger
3 cups cooked brown rice
1 cup chopped celery
$\frac{1}{2}$ cup mayonnaise
$\frac{1}{2}$ teaspoon curry powder
salt and pepper
slices of lemon and paprika pepper for garnish

Peel, core and dice apple. Place all ingredients in a bowl and mix together, adjust seasoning if necessary and chill.

To serve, place in a salad bowl, garnish with slices of lemon and sprinkle with a little paprika pepper.

Tomato Avocado Cups

Serves: 4

4 firm tomatoes
1 large avocado pear
$\frac{1}{2}$ cup chopped pimientos
salt and pepper
1 teaspoon lemon juice
$\frac{1}{2}$ small onion, chopped
few drops Tabasco sauce

Cut a slice from the top of each tomato, scoop out centre and place in a bowl.

Skin avocado pear, remove stone and add to tomato pulp with remaining ingredients. Mix together thoroughly, adjust seasoning and fill tomato cases. Chill before serving.

Delicious served with Russian Potato Salad (see page 72).

Tropical Fiesta Salad

Serves: 6–8

1 large pineapple
2 oranges
2 pears
1 cup strawberries or raspberries
½ cup sliced peaches
1 cup seedless white grapes
4 tablespoons honey
juice of 1 lemon
stoned cherries for decoration

Cut pineapple in half lengthways, cutting through leaves and down to stalk end. Scoop out pineapple flesh and cut into bite-size pieces. Peel oranges and cut into segments. Peel, core and slice pears. Cut strawberries in halves if large.

Combine pineapple, oranges, pears, strawberries, peaches and grapes in a large bowl. Add honey and lemon juice. Mix together thoroughly, being careful not to break fruit, chill.

To serve, place fruit salad in pineapple skins and decorate with cherries.

Dips,
Dressings,
Sauces

Avocado Savoury

2 ripe avocado pears
1 small ripe tomato, finely chopped
1 small onion, skinned and finely chopped
1 clove garlic, crushed
1 tablespoon lemon juice
few drops Tabasco sauce
salt and pepper
pieces of crisp vegetables, small savoury biscuits or croûtes for serving

Skin avocado pears, remove stones and place in a mixing bowl. Add remaining ingredients and beat together thoroughly. Adjust seasoning if necessary and chill.

Serve as a dip with pieces of crisp vegetables or spread on small savoury biscuits or croûtes.

Eggplant Savoury

1 eggplant
$\frac{1}{4}$ cup salad oil
2 onions, chopped
3 bay leaves
3 carrots, chopped
$\frac{1}{4}$ cabbage, finely shredded
6 tomatoes, chopped
salt and pepper

Place eggplant in a saucepan of boiling water and cook for approximately 15 minutes or until tender. Drain and cool. Remove skin from eggplant, place in a bowl and mash with a fork.

In a large saucepan, heat oil and fry onions until golden. Add bay leaves and carrots, cover and cook for 20 minutes. Add cabbage, tomatoes and salt and pepper to taste, cook for a further 10 minutes.

Combine with eggplant and serve hot, or cool and serve as a savoury dip or spread.

Fruit Salad Dressing

1 cup mayonnaise
$\frac{1}{2}$ cup mashed banana
$\frac{1}{4}$ cup desiccated coconut
$\frac{1}{2}$ cup crushed pineapple

Combine all ingredients in a bowl and mix together thoroughly. Serve with fruit salads.

French Dressing

1 clove garlic, crushed
3 tablespoons salad oil
pinch of black pepper
$\frac{1}{4}$ teaspoon salt
1 tablespoon lemon juice
$\frac{1}{2}$ teaspoon dry mustard

Place all ingredients in a screw-top jar, shake vigorously. Use as required.

TROPICAL FIESTA SALAD

Yoghurt Fruit Salad Dressing

1 cup yoghurt
2 teaspoons honey
$\frac{1}{4}$ teaspoon freshly grated nutmeg
$\frac{1}{4}$ teaspoon ground cinnamon
$\frac{1}{4}$ teaspoon ground ginger
$\frac{1}{2}$ teaspoon grated lemon rind
fresh fruit salad or stewed fruit for serving

Mix all ingredients together and chill well. Serve over prepared fruit.

Note: Desiccated coconut may be sprinkled over the top of each dessert before serving.

Mayonnaise

1 tablespoon sugar or honey
$\frac{1}{2}$ teaspoon dry mustard
$\frac{1}{2}$ teaspoon paprika pepper
salt and pepper
$\frac{1}{2}$ cup evaporated milk
$2\frac{1}{2}$ tablespoons vinegar
$1\frac{1}{4}$ cups salad oil

Place sugar, mustard, paprika pepper and salt and pepper in a small mixing bowl, gradually add evaporated milk, beating thoroughly. Add vinegar and oil alternately, beating well after each addition. Adjust seasoning if necessary.

Serve with salads.

Almond Sauce

½ cup chopped blanched almonds
2 tablespoons vegetable oil
1 cup hot water
1 tablespoon cornflour
¼ teaspoon salt
2 teaspoons lemon juice

Heat oil in a small saucepan, add almonds and cook until golden brown. Add cornflour, blend until smooth. Pour in water and stirring continuously, bring to the boil and simmer 2-3 minutes. Add salt and lemon juice.

Serve immediately with hot vegetables or chill and serve with salads.

Brown Gravy

2 good tablespoons (1 oz) plain wholemeal flour
1 teaspoon Parisian essence or soya bean sauce
salt and pepper
$\frac{1}{2}$ onion, finely chopped
$1\frac{1}{2}$ cups water, stock or vegetable liquor
2 tablespoons vegetable oil

Heat oil in a small saucepan, fry onion until golden brown. Add flour and blend until smooth. Cook for 2 minutes. Add water, Parisian essence and salt and pepper to taste and stirring continuously, bring to the boil. Simmer gently for 5 minutes.

Strain and serve with vegetable dishes.

Tomato Cream Sauce

½ onion, finely chopped
1 tablespoon vegetable oil
1 × 8 oz can condensed tomato soup
2 bay leaves
1 tablespoon Worcestershire sauce
salt and pepper
2 tablespoons sour cream

Fry onion in oil until golden brown. Add tomato soup, bay leaves, Worcestershire sauce and salt and pepper. Simmer for 10 minutes. Remove bay leaves, fold in sour cream and adjust seasoning if necessary.

Serve hot with vegetable dishes, delicious with cabbage or spinach.

White Lemon Sauce

1 oz butter or margarine
$\frac{1}{2}$ white onion, finely chopped
2 good tablespoons (1 oz) plain flour
juice of $\frac{1}{2}$ lemon
$\frac{1}{2}$ teaspoon salt
freshly ground pepper
$1\frac{1}{4}$ cups milk

Melt butter in a small saucepan, add onion and fry
until golden. Add flour and blend until smooth.
Stir over gentle heat for 1–2 minutes. Add milk
and salt and pepper to taste. Stirring continuously,
bring to the boil, simmer for 1–2 minutes.
Add lemon juice and serve with vegetable dishes.

Desserts,
Cakes,
Biscuits

Aloha Dessert

Serves: 4–6

1 pineapple
1 cup raisins
1 cup cherries, stoned
2 eating apples, chopped
1 cup desiccated coconut
3 persimmons
1 cup pineapple juice
1 eating apple, grated
1 tablespoon finely chopped mint
extra cherries for decoration

Slice pineapple in half lengthways, cutting through leaves and down to stalk end. Scoop out pineapple flesh and cut into bite-size pieces. Place pineapple, raisins, cherries, chopped apple and coconut in a bowl. Cut persimmons in halves and scoop out flesh, add to other fruits, mix thoroughly.

Mix pineapple juice, grated apple and chopped mint together and pour over fruit salad, chill.

To serve, spoon fruit salad into pineapple skins and decorate with extra cherries.

Apple Compote

Serves: 4

6 cooking apples
⅔ cup sultanas
4 tablespoons water
5 tablespoons (2 oz) raw sugar
2 cloves
freshly grated nutmeg
custard or cream for serving

Peel, core and slice apples. Place in a saucepan with sultanas, water, sugar and cloves. Cover pan tightly and simmer fruit gently until tender. Remove cloves and sprinkle with nutmeg.

When cool, serve with custard or cream.

Cottage Cheese with Fruit

Serves: 4

1 cup cottage cheese
2 teaspoons grated orange rind
12 strawberries
2 oranges, sliced
8 oz seedless white grapes
1 small pawpaw or rockmelon, sliced
icing sugar

Mix cottage cheese and orange rind together. Divide into 4 portions and place in the centre of each plate. Arrange prepared fruit around the cheese and serve sprinkled with icing sugar.

Chilled German Dessert

Serves: 4

1½ cups raspberries or other berry fruit
1½ cups cream
2 oz block chocolate, grated (preferably dark)

Reserve 4 whole raspberries for decoration.

Whip cream until thick, fold in chocolate and remaining raspberries. Place in glass serving dishes and chill.

Top with reserved raspberries before serving.

European Compote

Serves: 4–6

1 cup dried apricots
1 cup dried apples
1 cup prunes, stoned
5 cups cold water
1 tablespoon ($\frac{1}{2}$ oz) raw sugar
1 × $3\frac{1}{4}$ oz packet raspberry jelly crystals
1 cup boiling water
1 tablespoon cornflour mixed with 1 tablespoon water
vanilla ice cream or whipped cream for serving

Soak apricots, apples and prunes in cold water overnight.

In the morning, place in a saucepan with sugar, bring to the boil and simmer for approximately 15 minutes or until fruits are tender.

Dissolve jelly crystals in boiling water, add to stewed fruits with cornflour mixture. Bring to the boil, stirring continuously. Simmer 2–3 minutes, cool. Serve compote with ice cream or whipped cream.

Combination Fruit Dessert

Serves: 4

2 pears
2 bananas
12 strawberries
1 cup cottage cheese
2 tablespoons desiccated coconut
2 tablespoons honey
1 teaspoon ground cinnamon
1¼ cups cream
1 teaspoon coffee essence

Peel and core pears, cut into chunks. Peel and slice bananas. Wash strawberries and cut in halves. Combine fruits with cottage cheese, coconut, honey and cinnamon. Place in a serving dish and chill.

Whip cream and fold in coffee essence, pour over dessert and serve.

Fresh Fruit Salad

Serves: 4

2 eating apples
1 banana
1 orange
¼ pawpaw
4 passionfruit
4 slices pineapple
juice of 1 lemon
icing sugar
ice cream for serving

Peel, core and slice apples. Peel and slice banana and orange. Remove skin and seeds from pawpaw and cut into pieces. Remove pulp from passionfruit and cut pineapple into pieces.

Combine all fruits in a large serving bowl, pour over lemon juice and add icing sugar according to taste. Mix thoroughly and serve with vanilla ice cream.

Caramelised Grapes

Serves: 4

$1-1\frac{1}{2}$ lb seedless white grapes
$1\frac{1}{4}$ cups cream
$\frac{1}{2}$ cup (3 oz) raw sugar

Wash grapes, remove from stalks. Place in an even layer in a flameproof serving dish. Whip cream until thick and cover grapes, smooth surface with a spatula. Sprinkle sugar evenly over cream.

Place under a hot grill, at least 3—inches from heat. Grill until sugar bubbles and caramelises. Cool, place in refrigerator and chill until ready to serve.

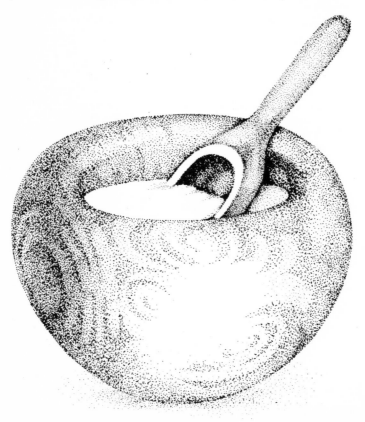

Prune Compote

Serves: 4

1 cup prune juice
1 tablespoon cornflour
2 tablespoons honey
1 tablespoon ($\frac{1}{2}$ oz) raw sugar
1 cup stoned, chopped prunes
$\frac{1}{2}$ oz butter or margarine
3 tablespoons lemon juice
pinch of salt
whipped cream for serving

Mix a little of the prune juice with cornflour, blend until smooth. In a saucepan, heat remaining prune juice with honey. Add blended cornflour and stirring continuously, bring to the boil, simmer for 5 minutes. Add sugar and prunes and cook for a further 5 minutes. Remove from heat and add butter, lemon juice and salt, mix thoroughly.

Serve warm or cold with whipped cream.

Russian Festival Dessert

Serves: 6–8

1 cup seedless raisins
1 tablespoon hot water
½ cup mixed glacé fruits
1 lb cream cheese
1¼ cups sour cream
1 cup (7 oz) castor sugar
½ teaspoon almond essence
½ teaspoon vanilla essence
chopped blanched almonds and glacé cherries for decoration

Place raisins in a bowl and add water, stand for 30 minutes. Finely chop glacé fruits. Beat cream cheese, sour cream, sugar, almond essence and vanilla essence together until smooth. Add glacé fruits and raisins, mix thoroughly.

Place in a glass serving bowl, chill overnight. Before serving, decorate with chopped almonds and glacé cherries.

CLOCKWISE: CHILLED GERMAN DESSERT
EUROPEAN COMPOTE. RUSSIAN FESTIVAL DESSERT

APPLE CRUMBLE
AND WHIPPED CREAM

Apple Crumble

Time: 1 hour
Temperature: 375–400°F
Serves: 6

6 cooking apples
3 cloves
$\frac{1}{2}$ cup honey
1 cup (4 oz) plain wholemeal flour
1 cup oatmeal
$\frac{1}{4}$ cup wheat germ
$\frac{1}{4}$ teaspoon salt
$\frac{1}{2}$ cup (3 oz) raw sugar
6 oz butter or margarine
whipped cream or custard for serving

Peel, core and slice apples, place in an ovenproof dish. Add cloves and pour over honey.

Place flour, oatmeal, wheat germ, salt and sugar in a mixing bowl. Rub in butter until mixture is crumbly, spread over apples.

Bake in a moderately hot oven for 1 hour or until top is golden brown. Serve with whipped cream or custard.

Apple Dessert Cake

Time: 25–30 minutes
Temperature: 350–375 °F

2 cups (8 oz) plain wholemeal flour
3 teaspoons baking powder
1 teaspoon salt
2 oz butter or margarine
2 good tablespoons (1 oz) raw sugar
½ cup grated Cheddar cheese
¾ cup milk
3 cups apple pulp
extra 1 oz butter or margarine
custard or cream for serving

Topping:
⅓ cup (2 oz) raw sugar
1 teaspoon coffee essence
½ teaspoon ground cinnamon

Grease a 7 × 12 × 1–inch Swiss roll tin.

Sieve flour, baking powder and salt into a mixing
bowl. Melt butter and mix with sugar and cheese.
Add to sieved dry ingredients with milk and apple.
Place in prepared Swiss roll tin, sprinkle topping
over cake. Dot with small pieces of extra butter.
Bake in a moderate oven for 25–30 minutes or
until cooked. Serve warm or cold with custard or
cream.

Topping: Mix sugar, coffee essence and cinnamon
together.

Banana Pudding

Time: 2–2½ hours
Temperature: 300–325°F
Serves: 4

3 oz brown rice
4 bananas
5 cups milk
1 cup honey
1 cup raisins
grated rind of 1 lemon

Wash rice in cold water. Mash bananas and combine with rice in a greased baking dish. Add milk, honey, raisins and lemon rind, mix well.

Cook in a slow oven for 2–2½ hours, stir occasionally. When rice is tender, remove from oven, cool and serve.

Fruit Cake

Time: 1¼ hours
Temperature: 350–375°F

1 cup (6 oz) raw sugar
1½ cups chopped walnuts
1 cup raisins
½ oz butter or margarine
1 teaspoon ground cinnamon
¼ teaspoon ground cloves
¼ teaspoon ground nutmeg
1 cup water
1½ cups mixed dried fruits
1 cup glacé cherries, halved
½ cup chopped blanched almonds
extra ¼ cup water
1 teaspoon bicarbonate of soda
2 cups (8 oz) plain wholemeal flour
4 teaspoons baking powder
pinch of salt

Line and grease an 8–inch round cake tin.

Place sugar, walnuts, raisins, butter, cinnamon, cloves, nutmeg and water in a saucepan, boil for 5 minutes. Add dried fruits, cherries and almonds, mix well and cool.

Bring extra water to the boil, add bicarbonate of soda and dissolve, add to mixture. Fold in sieved flour, baking powder and salt. Place mixture in prepared cake tin and bake in a moderate oven for approximately 1¼ hours or until cooked. Turn out of cake tin and cool on a wire cooling tray.

Raisin Nut Tea Loaf

Time: 1 hour
Temperature: 350–375°F

1 cup raisins
1 cup (6 oz) raw sugar or honey
1 tablespoon golden syrup
$\frac{1}{2}$ oz butter or margarine
1 tablespoon mixed spice
$\frac{1}{2}$ teaspoon ground ginger
1 cup cold water
$2\frac{1}{4}$ cups (10 oz) plain wholemeal flour
pinch of salt
2 teaspoons bicarbonate of soda
$\frac{1}{2}$ cup chopped walnuts or blanched almonds

Line and grease a 5 × 9–inch cake tin.

Place raisins, sugar, golden syrup, butter, spices and water in a saucepan, bring to the boil, cool.

When cold, add sieved flour, salt and bicarbonate of soda, mix together thoroughly. Fold in nuts and place mixture in prepared cake tin. Bake in a moderate oven for $1–1\frac{1}{4}$ hours or until cooked. Turn out of cake tin and cool on a wire cooling tray.

Store for one day before slicing and spreading with butter.

Candy Crunch

Time: 20–30 minutes
Temperature: 350–375 °F
Yield: 24

1 cup rolled oats
1 cup desiccated coconut
½ cup (3 oz) raw sugar
½ teaspoon vanilla essence
4 oz butter or margarine, melted

Grease a 7 × 12 × 1–inch Swiss roll tin.

Place rolled oats, coconut, sugar and vanilla essence in a mixing bowl. Add butter and mix together thoroughly.

Spread mixture evenly into prepared Swiss roll tin and bake in a moderate oven for 20–30 minutes. Cut into squares while hot.

When cool, remove from tin and store in an airtight container.

Oatmeal Biscuits

Time: 20–25 minutes
Temperature: 350–375°F
Yield: 24

4 oz butter or margarine
$\frac{1}{3}$ cup (2 oz) raw sugar
1 cup (4 oz) plain wholemeal flour
pinch of salt
4 oz fine oatmeal
$\frac{1}{4}$ cup milk
2 oz blanched almonds, finely chopped

Cream butter and sugar together in a mixing bowl.
Add sieved flour, salt and oatmeal. Add milk and
mix to a firm dough.

Press mixture into a greased 7 × 12 × 1–inch Swiss
roll tin and sprinkle with almonds. Bake in a
moderate oven for 20–25 minutes or until golden
brown. When cool, cut into squares and remove
from tin.

Summer
Menus

SPRING SALAD
TOSSED GREEN SALAD
ANISEED SALAD (FINOCCHIO)

COFFEE MOUSSE

Spring Salad

Serves: 4

2 × 16 oz cans garbanzos beans
6 firm tomatoes, chopped
8 oz French beans, cooked and sliced
1 white onion, sliced
2 oz blanched almonds, finely chopped
juice of $\frac{1}{2}$ lemon
salt and pepper
lettuce for serving
sprigs of watercress for garnish

Place garbanzos beans, tomatoes, French beans
and onion in a large mixing bowl, sprinkle with
almonds and lemon juice. Season to taste with salt
and pepper, toss together gently and chill.

Serve on a bed of lettuce and garnish with sprigs of
watercress.

Tossed Green Salad

Serves: 4

1 lettuce
1 cucumber, peeled
1 clove garlic
6 spring onions, chopped
2 stalks celery, sliced
French Dressing (see page 80)

Wash lettuce and tear into bite–size pieces, dry thoroughly. Thinly slice cucumber. Rub wooden salad bowl with cut clove of garlic. Place prepared vegetables in salad bowl and pour over French Dressing. Toss gently together and serve immediately.

Aniseed Salad

(Finocchio)

Serves: 4

3–4 aniseed

Dressing:
3 tablespoons salad oil
1 tablespoon lemon juice
salt
freshly ground pepper

Wash and trim aniseed, slice thinly, place in a wooden salad bowl. Pour dressing over, toss well and serve immediately.

Dressing: Combine all ingredients in a screw-top jar, shake vigorously.

Coffee Mousse

Serves: 4

$\frac{1}{2}$ cup cold water
1 oz gelatine
1 × 14$\frac{1}{2}$ oz can evaporated milk
1 tablespoon instant coffee
$\frac{1}{2}$ teaspoon vanilla essence
2 tablespoons (1 oz) castor sugar
whipped cream for decoration

Pour water into a small saucepan, sprinkle gelatine over and heat gently until gelatine dissolves. Add 1 cup of evaporated milk, instant coffee, vanilla essence and sugar. Mix well and chill until mixture begins to thicken.

Meanwhile, pour remaining evaporated milk into a refrigerator tray and freeze until ice crystals begin to form around edges. Place in a mixing bowl and beat until it begins to thicken, add gelatine mixture and continue to beat until thick. Pour into a serving dish and chill.

Decorate with cream before serving.

Legume Salad

Serves: 6–8

1 cup bean sprouts, drained
8 oz butter beans, cooked
4 stalks celery, chopped
$\frac{1}{4}$ cabbage, finely shredded
1 cup black olives, stoned
4 firm tomatoes, sliced
lettuce and sliced radishes for serving

Dressing:
4 tablespoons soya bean oil
juice of $\frac{1}{2}$ lemon
salt and pepper

Place prepared vegetables in a large bowl. Pour dressing over and mix together gently, chill.

Serve salad on a bed of lettuce and garnish with sliced radishes.

Dressing: Place all ingredients in a screw-top jar, shake vigorously.

Oriental Salad

Serves: 4

8 potatoes, cooked
1 × 13 oz can button mushrooms
1 × 14 oz can artichoke hearts
walnut halves for garnish

Dressing:
4 tablespoons white wine vinegar
juice of $\frac{1}{2}$ lemon
salt and pepper
$\frac{1}{4}$ cup coarsely chopped parsley
pinch of dried dill
pinch of ground mace

Slice potatoes, place in a salad bowl, pour over dressing.

Drain and slice mushrooms and artichokes. Gently mix with potatoes. Garnish with walnut halves before serving.

Dressing: Mix all ingredients together thoroughly.

French Salad

Serves: 4

1 lettuce
1 clove garlic, halved
French Dressing (see page 80)

Wash and dry lettuce, tear into bite-size pieces.

Rub wooden salad bowl with cut clove of garlic, place lettuce in bowl. Before serving, add French Dressing and toss together thoroughly.

Tahitian Exotica

Serves: 4

4 bananas
$\frac{1}{2}$ pawpaw
$\frac{1}{2}$ pineapple
2 small mangos
juice of 1 lemon
6 passionfruit

Peel and slice bananas. Remove skin and seeds from pawpaw, cut into chunks. Skin pineapple, discard core and cut into chunks. Remove skin from mangos, stone and cut into pieces. In a bowl, combine fruits with lemon juice, chill.

Serve in coconut shells, topped with passionfruit pulp.

Winter
Menus

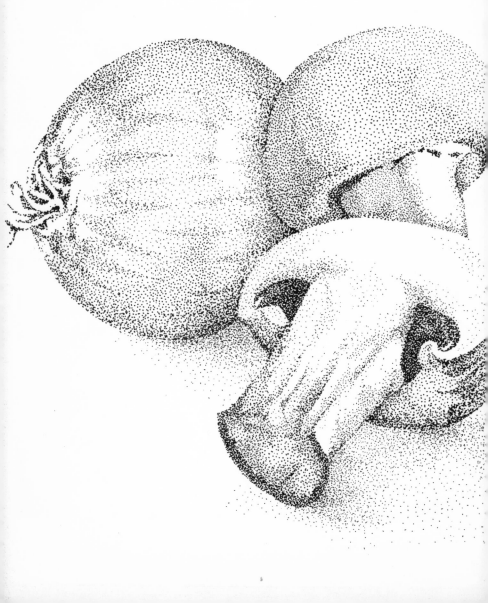

TOP TO BOTTOM: OATMEAL BISCUITS
RAISIN NUT TEA LOAF, CANDY CRUNCH

Mushroom Stroganoff

Serves: 4

2 × 16 oz cans meat substitute patties
2 oz butter or margarine
12 spring onions, chopped
2 lb mushrooms, sliced
1 packet dehydrated onion soup
1 tablespoon paprika pepper
2 cups sour cream
finely chopped parsley for garnish

Slice meat substitute patties into strips.

Heat butter in a large frying pan and sauté meat
substitute, spring onions and mushrooms, mix
together carefully. Add onion soup and cook for
10 minutes. Add paprika pepper and sour cream and
cook for a further 10 minutes. Garnish with parsley
before serving.

Potato Casserole

Time: 30 minutes
Temperature: 350–375 °F
Serves: 4

8 potatoes
butter or margarine
milk
salt and pepper

Peel potatoes and cook in boiling salted water for approximately 20 minutes or until tender. Drain thoroughly and mash, adding enough butter and milk to cream potatoes. (For each 1 lb of potatoes allow approximately 2 tablespoons milk and 1 oz butter). Add salt and pepper to taste.

Place potatoes in a greased ovenproof casserole. Cook in a moderate oven for approximately 30 minutes or until lightly browned on top.

Baked Apples

Time: 45 minutes–1 hour
Temperature: 350–375 °F
Serves: 4

4 cooking apples
8 prunes, stoned
2 tablespoons raisins
4 tablespoons honey
1 oz butter or margarine
4 tablespoons water
custard for serving

Remove cores from apples. Chop prunes and combine with raisins, stuff apples and place in a baking dish. Pour honey over apples and dot with butter. Add water to baking dish.

Bake in a moderate oven for 45 minutes–1 hour or until apples are tender. Serve hot with custard.

Spaghetti Milano

Serves: 4

2 green peppers
3 stalks celery
2 oz butter or margarine
12 spring onions, chopped
2 cloves garlic, crushed
6 ripe tomatoes, chopped
1 × 15 oz can mince meat substitue
pinch of dried oregano
salt and pepper
1 × 12 oz packet wholemeal spaghetti
grated Parmesan cheese for serving

Seed and chop peppers, slice celery.

Heat butter in a saucepan, sauté spring onions and garlic until golden. Add peppers and celery, cook gently for 10 minutes. Add tomatoes and cook for a further 15 minutes or until pepper is tender. Crumble mince meat substitute and add to sauce with oregano and salt and pepper to taste.

Meanwhile, cook spaghetti in a large saucepan of boiling water until just tender, drain.

Serve sauce over hot spaghetti and sprinkle with Parmesan cheese.

French Beans with Lemon

Serves: 4

1 lb French beans, sliced
½ oz butter or margarine
1 tablespoon lemon juice
salt
freshly ground pepper

Cook beans in boiling salted water for 8–10 minutes or until just tender. Drain thoroughly. Add butter, lemon juice and season to taste with salt and pepper.

Toss gently together and serve immediately.

Melon and Strawberries

Serves: 4

1 rockmelon
1 box strawberries
whipped cream for serving

Cut rockmelon in half, discard seeds. Remove flesh with a melon ball scoop and place in a bowl. Hull strawberries and wash (cut in halves if large), add to rockmelon and mix together.

Chill fruit and serve with cream.

Spanish Rice

Time: 30 minutes
Temperature: 350–375 °F
Serves: 4

3 cups brown rice
vegetable oil for frying
1 large onion, finely chopped
1 red pepper, seeded and chopped
2 cups canned tomatoes
1 lb mushrooms, sliced
$\frac{1}{2}$ teaspoon salt
freshly ground pepper

Cook rice in boiling salted water until just tender, drain.

Heat oil in a saucepan and sauté onion and pepper until onion is golden. Add tomatoes and mushrooms and season to taste with salt and pepper. Simmer gently for 5–10 minutes. Add rice and mix together.

Place in a greased ovenproof casserole and cook in a moderate oven for approximately 30 minutes or until hot. Serve immediately.

Spinach with Lemon

Serves: 4

1 bunch spinach
salt and pepper
2 oz butter or margarine
1 tablespoon lemon juice

Wash and shred spinach. Cook in boiling salted water for 10 minutes or until tender. Drain thoroughly and replace in dry saucepan. Season to taste with salt and pepper. Add butter and lemon juice and toss together.

Serve as a vegetable or on hot buttered toast.

Avocado Cream Cheese

Serves: 4

2 avocado pears
4 small bananas
12 oz cream cheese
2 tablespoons desiccated coconut
1 teaspoon ground cinnamon
2 tablespoons (1 oz) castor sugar
2 teaspoons coffee essence
$1\frac{1}{4}$ cups cream

Peel avocado pears, remove stones and cut into chunks. Peel bananas and slice thinly. Cut cream cheese into $\frac{1}{2}$—inch pieces. Combine avocado pears, bananas, cream cheese, coconut, cinnamon and sugar. Mix carefully and chill.

Mix coffee essence and cream together, pour over combined fruits and cheese. Serve immediately.

Note: Cream may be semi-whipped if desired.

Vegetable Chop Suey

Serves: 4

1 × 15 oz can soya meat
8 oz mushrooms, sliced
2 tablespoons vinegar
3 tablespoons water
salt and pepper
1½ oz butter or margarine
2 large onions, chopped
1 × 12 oz can bamboo shoots, drained
pinch of ground mixed spice
1 teaspoon raw sugar
1 teaspoon soya sauce
soya sauce and sweet relish for serving

Cut soya meat into small pieces. Place in a bowl
with mushrooms and add vinegar, water and salt
and pepper to taste. Stand for approximately 1 hour.

Meanwhile, heat butter in a frying pan, add onions
and sauté until golden. Add bamboo shoots and
cook for 5 minutes. Add soya meat mixture, mixed
spice, sugar and soya sauce. Mix thoroughly and
cook for a further 10 minutes or until hot.

Serve with soya sauce and sweet relish.

Taiwan Fried Rice

Serves: 4

2 oz butter or margarine
6 spring onions, chopped
2 stalks celery, chopped
2 peppers, seeded and chopped
1 teaspoon soya sauce
6 cups cooked brown rice
salt and pepper
3 tablespoons finely chopped parsley for garnish

Heat butter in a large frying pan, add spring onions, celery and peppers, sauté until pepper is soft. Add soya sauce, rice and salt and pepper to taste, fry for 10 minutes.

Garnish with finely chopped parsley and serve immediately.

Chinese Pears

Time: 30 minutes
Temperature: 350–375 °F
Serves: 4

4 ripe pears
2 oz walnuts, chopped
4 tablespoons honey
1 teaspoon ground ginger
cream or ice cream for serving

Peel and core pears, place in a greased baking dish. Fill centres with walnuts and honey, sprinkle with ground ginger.

Bake in a moderate oven for approximately 30 minutes or until tender. Serve with cream or ice cream

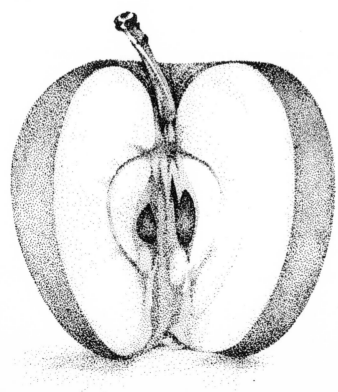

Terms used in
Natural Foods Cookbook

Castor sugar	:	Finely ground white sugar
Cornflour	:	Cornstarch
Eggplant	:	Aubergine
French beans	:	Green beans, string beans
Frying pan	:	Skillet
Grill	:	To broil
Icing sugar	:	Confectioners' sugar
Pawpaw	:	Papaya
Pepper	:	Capsicum
Plain flour	:	All-purpose flour
Raw sugar	:	Honey-coloured crystals
Rockmelon	:	Canteloupe
Spring onion	:	Shallot or scallion
Stock cube	:	Bouillon cube
Zucchini	:	Courgette

Acknowledgements

The editor would like to thank the following for their help and co-operation in the preparation of and photography for this book:

Ember Ware Sales Co., Balmain
Giftmaker, Paddington
Sanitarium Health Food Company
The Bay Tree Kitchen Shop, Woollahra
The Wedgwood, Double Bay

124

To my mother and husband for their
help, and to all those who wish
to lead a better and healthful life.

Index